INFOQUAKE

Navigating the Revolution of Instant Knowledge

Isabelle Hartley

Copyright Copy

All content in this book is protected under copyright laws. Any reproduction, distribution, or unauthorized use of any part of this book without the prior written consent of the copyright owner is strictly prohibited except for personal use.

TABLE OF CONTENT

iii

Chapter 1: The Digital Deluge

Adapting to the Information Onslaught

In our digital age, information flows ceaselessly, flooding our lives with a constant stream of data. This deluge of information, while empowering, also poses significant challenges. How we navigate and harness this torrent directly impacts our ability to thrive in a rapidly changing world. In this chapter, we delve into the very nature of this information overload, dissecting its effects on our daily lives. We will explore the importance of understanding and managing this inundation, providing valuable insights and strategies to help you not only survive but thrive amidst the relentless waves of information.

Understanding the Information Overload

In an era where information is more accessible than ever before, we find ourselves grappling with an unprecedented phenomenon - information overload. This chapter seeks to unravel the complexities of this digital deluge and explore how it impacts our lives.

Information overload occurs when the volume of information available exceeds our capacity to absorb, process, and make sense of it. With the internet, social media, 24/7 news cycles, and the constant connectivity of modern life, we are bombarded with information from every direction. Emails, notifications, news updates, and social media feeds demand our attention, often simultaneously.

The consequences of information overload can be profound. It can lead to stress, anxiety, and decision fatigue. When inundated with too much information, our ability to focus diminishes, and our productivity suffers. We become easily distracted, perpetually skimming the surface of topics, but rarely diving deep. In this state, critical thinking and discernment become casualties.

To navigate this digital maelstrom effectively, it's crucial to recognize the signs of information overload in your life. Do you constantly check your phone? Feel overwhelmed by your inbox? Struggle to keep up with the latest news or trends? These are all indicators that you may be experiencing information overload.

The good news is that understanding information overload is the first step toward regaining control. By acknowledging its presence and impact, you can start to implement strategies to mitigate its effects. These strategies may include setting boundaries on your information consumption, curating your sources to prioritize quality over quantity, and learning to disconnect periodically to allow your mind to recharge.

In the chapters that follow, we will explore practical techniques for managing this deluge of information. From effective filtering and accelerated learning methods to digital organization and maintaining a healthy information diet, you will gain the tools and insights needed to not only survive but thrive in the age of information overload. Embrace the journey to regain control over your information consumption, and you'll find that in doing so, you regain control over your life.

Assessing the Impact on Your Life

The relentless influx of information in the digital age doesn't just influence the way we gather knowledge; it profoundly shapes our lives, habits, and well-being. To navigate this era of information overload effectively, it's crucial to pause and assess its impact on your life. Only by understanding the consequences can you take meaningful steps toward managing this digital deluge.

- Stress and Anxiety: Information overload can be a significant source of stress and anxiety. The constant bombardment of news, notifications, and messages can leave you feeling overwhelmed and on edge. It's essential to recognize how this stress affects your mental and physical health. Are you losing sleep over the fear of missing out on news or messages? Do you often find yourself checking your devices anxiously? Assessing these patterns can reveal the toll of information overload on your well-being.

- Productivity and Focus: Information overload can be a productivity killer. Constant interruptions from emails, social media, and news alerts can make it challenging to concentrate on tasks at hand. As a result, you might find that you're less productive, taking longer to complete projects, and struggling to maintain your focus. Reflect on your work habits—do you frequently switch between tasks? Is your attention easily diverted by digital distractions?

- Relationships: The digital world's grip on our attention can also affect our relationships. Do you find yourself glued to your phone or computer when spending time with loved ones? Are face-to-face conversations interrupted by the ping of notifications? Assessing how information overload affects your interactions with friends and family can reveal the strain it places on your personal connections.

- Decision Making: Information overload can hinder your ability to make informed decisions. When overwhelmed by a constant stream of information, it's challenging to sift through the noise and discern what's relevant. Are you making impulsive decisions because you lack the time or mental clarity to thoroughly analyze information? Recognizing how this overload affects your decision-making processes is crucial.

- Learning and Growth: In the pursuit of information, we often sacrifice depth for breadth. Information overload can lead to superficial knowledge acquisition rather than deep learning. Assess whether you're skimming the surface of topics or genuinely absorbing and applying what you learn. Are you finding it challenging to engage in sustained, focused learning or deep work?

- Time Management: Efficiently managing your time becomes increasingly difficult in the face of information overload. The constant need to check emails, social media, and news can create a sense of urgency that disrupts your schedule and priorities. Reflect on how much time you spend on digital devices and whether it aligns with your goals and values.

As you assess the impact of information overload on your life, remember that the goal isn't to eliminate all digital engagement but to regain control. By understanding how information overload affects your stress levels, productivity, relationships, decision making, learning, and time management, you can take targeted steps to address these challenges.

In the chapters that follow, we will explore practical strategies to mitigate these negative effects. From setting boundaries on your digital consumption to developing critical thinking skills, you'll gain the tools needed to reclaim your time, focus, and well-being in the digital age. By assessing the impact of information overload, you're taking the first step toward a more balanced and fulfilling relationship with the digital world.

The Importance of Information Management

In a world where information is abundant and easily accessible, the ability to manage and organize this vast sea of data is becoming increasingly crucial. The term "information management" encompasses a wide range of practices, tools, and strategies aimed at collecting, storing, retrieving, and disseminating information effectively. Understanding the significance of information management is essential as it directly impacts our personal and professional lives.

Enhancing Decision-Making: One of the primary reasons information management is essential lies in its role in decision-making. In both personal and professional contexts, informed decisions are critical. Whether you're choosing a career path, making an investment, or deciding on a vacation destination, having access to well-organized and reliable information can significantly improve the quality of your choices. Effective information management ensures that the right data is available at the right time, facilitating better decision-making.

Boosting Productivity: Information management can significantly enhance productivity. When you can quickly locate the information you need, you save time and reduce frustration. In a professional setting, efficient information management can streamline workflows, reduce errors, and improve overall productivity. In your personal life, it can lead to a more organized and less stressful existence.

Reducing Information Overload: As discussed in previous chapters, information overload is a pervasive issue in our digital age. Effective information management serves as a shield against this deluge. By filtering, prioritizing, and organizing the information you encounter, you can avoid feeling overwhelmed. This, in turn, helps reduce stress and anxiety associated with information overload.

Knowledge Retention: Information management isn't just about acquiring data; it's also about retaining and utilizing knowledge. Through effective organization and documentation, you can ensure that valuable insights and experiences are preserved for future reference. This is particularly valuable in learning environments and professional settings where institutional knowledge is essential.

Collaboration and Communication: In both personal and professional relationships, effective communication is key. Information management systems and tools can facilitate seamless collaboration. Whether you're working on a team project or maintaining a family calendar, the ability to share and access information efficiently can improve coordination and strengthen relationships.

Privacy and Security: The importance of protecting sensitive information cannot be overstated. Information management extends to safeguarding your data from unauthorized access or data breaches. Implementing robust security measures and encryption protocols ensures that your personal and confidential information remains secure.

Strategic Planning: In business and strategic contexts, information management plays a pivotal role in planning and forecasting. Data-driven decision-making relies on the availability of accurate and up-to-date information. Organizations that excel in information management are better positioned to adapt to changing market conditions and stay competitive.

Innovation and Growth: Access to well-managed information can fuel innovation and growth. By analyzing trends, customer feedback, and market data, individuals and organizations can identify opportunities for improvement and innovation. This, in turn, can lead to business growth, improved products and services, and personal development.

In summary, information management is not merely a technical or administrative endeavor; it is a fundamental skill that influences the quality of our lives. Whether you're striving to make informed decisions, boost productivity, reduce stress, protect your privacy, or foster innovation, effective information management is the linchpin that can unlock these benefits. In the following chapters, we will delve into practical tips and strategies for mastering the art of information management, equipping you with the tools you need to thrive in our information-rich world.

Chapter 2: Filtering the Noise

Strategies for Effective Information Selection

In our data-driven world, the ability to discern valuable information from the overwhelming noise is a skill of paramount importance. Chapter 2 explores the art of filtering, a critical facet of information management. We dive deep into practical strategies for sifting through the digital clamor, identifying reliable sources, and honing your critical thinking abilities. With these tools in hand, you'll gain the power to separate the signal from the noise, ensuring that the information you encounter is not just abundant but genuinely meaningful and reliable.

Identifying Reliable Sources

In an age where information flows freely from countless channels, the ability to distinguish reliable sources from unreliable ones is an indispensable skill. Whether you're researching a topic, making decisions based on information, or simply seeking to stay informed, the trustworthiness of your sources profoundly impacts the accuracy and reliability of the information you receive. Here, we delve into key strategies for identifying reliable sources in a sea of digital data.

- Credible Publications and Institutions: Begin your quest for reliable information by seeking out established and credible publications, journals, and institutions. Peer-reviewed academic journals, respected news outlets, and government agencies often adhere to rigorous standards of fact-checking and accuracy. Look for the publication's history of reliability and their commitment to transparency.

- Author Expertise: Consider the qualifications and expertise of the author or contributor. In academic and professional contexts, experts in their field are often the most reliable sources. Check for the author's credentials, affiliations, and relevant experience. Be cautious when dealing with anonymous or unverified authors.

- Citations and References: Reliable sources often cite their own sources. When evaluating an article or report, look for a list of citations and references. This allows you to trace the information back to its origin and assess the credibility of the sources cited. A lack of citations can be a red flag.

- Peer Review: In academic research, peer-reviewed publications are held in high regard. Peer review involves experts in the field evaluating the quality and validity of a piece of work before it's published. While not foolproof, peer-reviewed articles are generally more reliable due to this rigorous review process.

- Editorial Standards: Trusted publications have strong editorial standards. They employ editors and fact-checkers who review content for accuracy and consistency. Investigate the publication's editorial policies and ethics to gauge their commitment to responsible journalism.

- Cross-Verification: To enhance reliability, cross-verify information across multiple sources. If multiple reputable sources corroborate a piece of information, it's more likely to be accurate. However, beware of echo chambers where the same information is circulated without independent verification.

- Bias Awareness: Recognize that all sources, even reputable ones, may carry some degree of bias. Be aware of the publication's potential biases and consider how they might influence the information presented.

To get a balanced view, consult sources with varying perspectives.

- Fact-Checking Organizations: Fact-checking organizations like Snopes, PolitiFact, and FactCheck.org play a crucial role in evaluating the accuracy of claims and statements. When in doubt, consult these organizations to verify the authenticity of information.

- Domain Expertise: In certain fields, domain-specific expertise is required to evaluate the reliability of sources. For example, medical information should ideally be assessed by medical professionals, while financial information might require input from experts in finance or economics.

- User Reviews and Feedback: Online user reviews and feedback can provide insights into the credibility of sources. However, exercise caution, as these can also be manipulated or biased. Consider the overall consensus and look for patterns in user feedback.

- Red Flags: Be vigilant for common red flags, such as sensationalist language, grammatical errors, excessive advertising, or a lack of transparency about the publication's ownership and mission. These indicators can signal unreliable sources.

In our digital age, where misinformation and disinformation abound, the ability to identify reliable sources is a vital skill for informed decision-making, academic research, and responsible citizenship. By applying these strategies and maintaining a discerning eye, you can navigate the information landscape with confidence, ensuring that the knowledge you acquire is based on a foundation of credibility and trustworthiness.

Developing Critical Thinking Skills

In a world awash with information, the ability to think critically is more crucial than ever. Critical thinking is the skill of systematically evaluating information, arguments, and ideas to make reasoned and informed decisions. It's a skill that empowers individuals to separate fact from fiction, identify biases, and draw logical conclusions. In this chapter, we explore the importance of developing critical thinking skills and provide practical strategies to enhance this vital cognitive ability.

The Significance of Critical Thinking

Enhanced Decision-Making: Critical thinking equips you with the tools to make better decisions. When faced with complex choices or conflicting information, it enables you to assess the evidence, consider alternatives, and arrive at well-informed conclusions. This is invaluable in both personal and professional contexts.

- Problem Solving: Critical thinking is at the core of effective problem-solving. It allows you to dissect complex issues, break them down into manageable components, and explore creative solutions. This skill is highly sought after in the workplace, as it enables individuals to tackle challenges with confidence.

- Identification of Bias: Critical thinking involves recognizing and mitigating bias. By critically analyzing information sources and arguments, you can identify hidden agendas, prejudice, or manipulation. This ability is crucial for media literacy and resisting the influence of misinformation.

- Effective Communication: Individuals with strong critical thinking skills are better communicators. They can articulate their ideas clearly, support their arguments with evidence, and engage in constructive debates. This skill enhances interpersonal relationships and fosters productive dialogue.

Continuous Learning: Critical thinking is a catalyst for lifelong learning. It encourages curiosity, intellectual growth, and adaptability. When you approach new information with a critical mindset, you're more likely to absorb knowledge deeply and retain it over time.

Practical Strategies for Developing Critical Thinking Skills

Question Everything: Cultivate a habit of curiosity by questioning information, assumptions, and conclusions. Ask "Why?" and "How?" regularly. Encourage yourself to explore the underlying rationale behind statements and claims.

- Seek Diverse Perspectives: Expose yourself to diverse viewpoints and opinions, even those you disagree with. Engaging with differing perspectives broadens your understanding and challenges your own biases.

- Analyze Information Sources: When encountering information, evaluate the credibility and reliability of the source. Consider the author's qualifications, potential biases, and the publication's reputation. Reliable sources are the foundation of critical thinking.

- Consider Evidence: Scrutinize the evidence presented in arguments or claims. Is it sufficient and relevant? Look for logical fallacies and weak reasoning. Avoid accepting statements at face value without supporting evidence.

- Practice Active Listening: When engaging in conversations or consuming content, practice active listening. This means fully concentrating on the speaker or content and seeking to understand their perspective before forming your response or judgment.

- Think in Systems: Understand that many issues are interconnected and influenced by multiple factors. Employ systems thinking to analyze complex problems and consider the broader context.

- Use Critical Thinking Tools: Utilize critical thinking frameworks and tools, such as the Socratic method, SWOT analysis, or the Five Whys technique, to systematically analyze and solve problems.

- Reflect and Evaluate: Regularly review your own thought processes and decisions. Did you make judgments based on emotions or cognitive biases? Identifying areas where critical thinking can be improved is a step toward growth.

- Engage in Discussions: Engage in thoughtful discussions and debates with others. Constructive dialogues expose you to different perspectives and encourage you to defend your own views, strengthening your critical thinking abilities.

- Read Widely: Cultivate a habit of reading diverse materials, including books, articles, and research papers. Reading widely exposes you to various writing styles, arguments, and evidence.

- Practice Problem-Solving: Solve puzzles, riddles, and complex problems as a form of mental exercise. These activities hone your analytical thinking and problem-solving skills.

Developing critical thinking skills is an ongoing process that pays dividends in all aspects of life. By fostering a critical mindset, you become better equipped to navigate the information landscape, make informed decisions, and engage in thoughtful discourse. In our era of abundant information, critical thinking is the compass that guides us toward clarity and understanding.

Setting Personal Information Filters

In an age of information abundance, setting personal information filters is akin to constructing a mental fortress to protect your cognitive space and maintain mental clarity. The ability to filter information effectively is vital for managing the overwhelming deluge of data that inundates our lives daily. This chapter explores the importance of establishing personal information filters and provides practical strategies for doing so.

The Significance of Personal Information Filters

- Information Overload Mitigation: Personal information filters act as a shield against information overload. They help you sift through the digital noise and focus on what's relevant and valuable. By curating the information you consume, you prevent overwhelm and reduce stress.

- Enhanced Decision-Making: Information filters streamline the decision-making process. When you're inundated with data, it can be challenging to make choices. By prioritizing information that aligns with your goals and values, you make decisions more efficiently.

- Time Management: Effective information filters save you time. When you spend less time sifting through irrelevant information, you free up valuable time for more meaningful pursuits. This can lead to increased productivity and improved work-life balance.

- Reduced Cognitive Load: Constant exposure to irrelevant or conflicting information can create cognitive fatigue. Personal information filters help reduce this load, allowing your mind to focus on what truly matters.

Practical Strategies for Setting Personal Information Filters

Define Your Objectives: Start by clarifying your goals and objectives. What do you want to achieve with the information you consume? Knowing your purpose provides a clear framework for filtering information.

- Establish Priorities: Determine your priorities in both personal and professional domains. What information is crucial for your success, well-being, or growth? Prioritize sources and topics accordingly.
- Curate Your Sources: Choose your information sources carefully. Select reputable and reliable sources that align with your objectives. Whether it's news, social media, or research materials, curate your sources to minimize exposure to unreliable or biased content.
- Set Time Limits: Allocate specific time slots for information consumption. By setting time limits, you prevent mindless scrolling and ensure that you only engage with information during designated periods.
- Unsubscribe and Unfollow: Review your email subscriptions, social media accounts, and notifications. Unsubscribe from irrelevant newsletters and unfollow accounts

that don't contribute to your objectives. This reduces digital clutter.

- Use Technology Wisely: Leverage technology to your advantage. Utilize content filters, ad blockers, and website blockers to reduce exposure to distracting or irrelevant content. Many apps and platforms offer customization options to tailor your experience.

- Filter by Keywords: Implement keyword filters to screen out unwanted content. For instance, you can filter news articles or social media posts based on specific keywords that align with your interests or values.

- Practice Mindfulness: Be mindful of your information consumption habits. Pay attention to how different types of information make you feel. If certain content consistently triggers negative emotions or stress, reconsider your exposure.

- Audit Your Information Diet: Regularly assess the types of information you consume. Are you balanced in your consumption of news, entertainment, and educational content? Adjust your diet as needed to maintain equilibrium.

- Seek Trusted Recommendations: Rely on recommendations from trusted sources or individuals in your network. If someone you respect recommends a book, article, or resource, it's more likely to be valuable to you.

- Limit Multitasking: Avoid multitasking while consuming information. Devote your full attention to the content at hand. Multitasking reduces comprehension and retention.

- Reevaluate Periodically: Information needs and priorities change over time. Periodically reassess your information filters to ensure they remain aligned with your current goals and interests.

Setting personal information filters is an ongoing process of refinement and adjustment. It requires mindfulness, self-awareness, and a commitment to preserving mental clarity in a world inundated with data. By tailoring your information consumption to your objectives and values, you empower yourself to make better decisions, manage your time effectively, and maintain a sense of balance in your information-rich life.

Chapter 3: Accelerated Learning

Techniques for Rapid Information Absorption

In a fast-paced world where knowledge is a valuable asset, the ability to learn quickly and effectively is a game-changer. This chapter is your guide to mastering the art of accelerated learning. We delve into practical techniques designed to boost your reading speed, comprehension, memory retention, and note-taking skills. With these tools at your disposal, you'll be equipped to absorb information at a remarkable pace, empowering you to stay ahead in your studies, work, and personal growth endeavors.

Speed Reading and Comprehension

In an era where information is abundant, the skill of speed reading has gained significance. Speed reading is not just about reading quickly; it's about reading efficiently, with the ability to comprehend and retain information effectively. This chapter explores the art of speed reading, offering insights and practical techniques to enhance your reading speed while maintaining comprehension.

The Importance of Speed Reading

- Time Savings: Speed reading enables you to cover more material in less time. In a world where time is a precious resource, the ability to read quickly can significantly boost productivity.

- Information Absorption: Speed readers can absorb vast amounts of information in a shorter time frame. This is particularly advantageous for students, researchers, and professionals who need to process large volumes of data.

- Improved Focus: Speed reading requires intense concentration. As a result, it can enhance your ability to focus, reducing distractions and increasing your reading stamina.

- Better Retention: Contrary to the misconception that speed reading sacrifices comprehension, proficient speed readers often have excellent comprehension skills. This is because speed reading techniques encourage active engagement with the text, leading to better retention.

Practical Techniques for Speed Reading
- Pre-Reading Preparation: Before diving into a text, take a moment to preview it. Scan headings, subheadings, and any visual aids

like graphs or illustrations. This provides a roadmap for your reading, helping you anticipate the structure and main points.

- Eliminate Subvocalization: Subvocalization is the habit of silently pronouncing each word as you read. To increase your reading speed, aim to reduce subvocalization. Instead, focus on processing phrases or groups of words at a time.

- Use a Pointer or Guide: A pointer, such as your finger or a pen, can help you maintain a steady pace and prevent regression (going back to re-read). Gently guide your pointer along the lines of text as you read.

- Expand Your Peripheral Vision: Train your peripheral vision to capture more words at once. Instead of fixating on a single word, aim to see groups of words or entire lines at once. This reduces the need for eye movement.

- Practice Speed Drills: Engage in speed reading drills to improve your reading speed progressively. Set a timer for a short duration, like one minute, and read as much as you can within that time. Over time, challenge yourself to increase your reading speed.

- Chunking: Group words together into meaningful chunks or phrases. Your brain can process chunks of information more efficiently than individual words. This technique enhances both speed and comprehension.

- Adjust Your Reading Speed: Recognize that not all material requires the same reading speed. Adjust your pace based on the complexity and importance of the text. Skim through less critical content and slow down for in-depth reading.

- Active Engagement: Stay engaged with the text by asking questions, summarizing paragraphs, or mentally paraphrasing. Active reading techniques enhance comprehension while maintaining speed.

- Reduce Backtracking: Resist the urge to go back and re-read sections unless absolutely necessary. Trust your initial comprehension, and keep moving forward.

- Regular Practice: Speed reading is a skill that improves with practice. Dedicate time each day to speed reading exercises and gradually apply it to your everyday reading materials.

Balancing Speed and Comprehension

While speed reading techniques can significantly increase your reading speed, it's essential to strike a balance between speed and comprehension. Rushing through text at the expense of understanding defeats the purpose of speed reading. Therefore, practice is key. As you become more proficient, you'll naturally find the right balance that suits your reading goals, whether it's quick information absorption or deep comprehension.

Speed reading is a valuable tool for anyone seeking to navigate the information-rich landscape of the modern world more efficiently. With practice and patience, you can harness this skill to save time, increase productivity, and absorb knowledge rapidly without sacrificing comprehension.

Memory Improvement Techniques

Memory is the gateway to knowledge, and improving your memory can enhance your learning abilities, problem-solving skills, and overall cognitive function. In this chapter, we explore memory improvement techniques that will help you retain information more effectively and recall it when needed.

The Significance of Memory Improvement

- Enhanced Learning: A strong memory facilitates faster and more efficient learning. When you can remember facts, concepts, and experiences, you build a solid foundation for acquiring new knowledge.

- Better Problem Solving: Memory plays a critical role in problem-solving. It allows you to draw on past experiences and information to find solutions to current challenges.

- Increased Productivity: Improved memory means you can recall tasks, deadlines, and important details more readily, leading to increased productivity and better time management.

- Confidence Boost: A reliable memory boosts your self-confidence. When you can recall information and experiences accurately, you feel more capable and self-assured.

Practical Memory Improvement Techniques

- Mnemonic Devices: Mnemonic devices are memory aids that help you remember information by associating it with something more memorable. Examples include acronyms, rhymes, and visual imagery. For instance, "ROYGBIV" helps remember the order of colors in a rainbow.

- Chunking: Divide information into smaller, more manageable chunks. For example, remembering a long string of numbers is easier when you break them into groups, like phone numbers or credit card numbers.

- Visualization: Create vivid mental images related to what you want to remember. The more detailed and memorable the image, the better you'll recall the associated information.

- Association: Connect new information to something you already know. This establishes links in your memory, making it easier to retrieve the new data when needed.

- Spaced Repetition: Instead of cramming, space out your study or review sessions. Revisit information at increasing intervals over time, reinforcing your memory more effectively.

- Mind Mapping: Use mind maps to visually organize information. This technique helps you see connections between ideas, making it easier to remember complex concepts.
- Narrative Storytelling: Turn information into a narrative or story. Stories are easier to remember because they create a logical structure for the information to fit into.
- Physical Exercise: Regular physical activity, especially aerobic exercise, has been shown to enhance memory and cognitive function. Exercise increases blood flow to the brain, which promotes brain health.
- Adequate Sleep: Quality sleep is crucial for memory consolidation. During deep sleep, the brain processes and stores information learned during the day.
- Healthy Diet: Proper nutrition supports brain health. Omega-3 fatty acids, antioxidants, and foods rich in vitamins and minerals can benefit memory.

- Stress Management: High stress levels can impair memory. Practice stress-reduction techniques such as mindfulness, meditation, or relaxation exercises to improve memory function.

- Social Interaction: Engaging in social activities and conversations stimulates your brain and promotes memory retention.

- Continuous Learning: Challenging your brain with new activities and learning experiences can improve memory and cognitive function. Activities like learning a new language or playing a musical instrument are excellent choices.

- Limit Distractions: When you need to remember something, minimize distractions and focus your attention on the task at hand. Distractions can disrupt the encoding process in memory.

- Teach or Share Information: Teaching others what you've learned is a powerful memory booster. Explaining concepts or information to someone else reinforces your understanding and retention.

Practicing Patience and Consistency

Improving memory is a gradual process that requires patience and consistent effort. These techniques may not yield instant results, but with time and practice, you'll notice a significant improvement in your memory capacity. Remember that everyone's memory is unique, and what works best for you may vary from others. Experiment with different techniques to discover which ones are most effective in enhancing your memory. By making memory improvement a part of your daily routine, you can unlock the full potential of your cognitive abilities.

Efficient Note-Taking Methods

Taking effective notes is a valuable skill that can significantly enhance your ability to learn, retain information, and stay organized. Whether you're a student, professional, or someone looking to improve their knowledge retention, mastering efficient note-taking methods is a powerful tool. In this chapter, we explore various note-taking techniques and strategies that will help you capture information effectively and make the most of your notes.

The Importance of Efficient Note-Taking

- Enhanced Learning: Taking notes actively engages your mind in the learning process. It helps you process and understand information better, leading to improved comprehension and retention.

- Organization: Well-organized notes act as a reference guide for future review. They help you locate and retrieve information quickly, reducing the time spent searching for crucial details.

- Clarification: Note-taking encourages you to clarify concepts and ideas as you record them. This process promotes a deeper understanding of the subject matter.

- Active Engagement: Engaging with the material while taking notes keeps you attentive and focused during lectures, presentations, or reading sessions. It minimizes distractions and enhances concentration.

- Critical Thinking: Effective note-taking requires you to extract key points and synthesize information. This cultivates critical thinking skills and the ability to identify essential information.

Practical Note-Taking Techniques

- The Cornell Method: Divide your note paper into three sections: a narrow left column for cues, a wider right column for notes, and a summary section at the bottom. During the lecture or reading, jot down main ideas and keywords in the right column. Afterward, use the cues to quiz yourself or create a summary in the bottom section.

- Outline Method: Create an outline format with headings, subheadings, and bullet points. This method is ideal for organizing hierarchical information and showing relationships between ideas.

- Mind Mapping; Use a visual approach to note-taking by creating mind maps. Start with a central idea or concept and branch out with related subtopics and keywords. Mind maps help visualize connections and are particularly useful for brainstorming and organizing complex information.

- Sentence Method: Write full sentences that capture the main points and details. This method can be more comprehensive but may require faster writing skills to keep up with the speaker.

- Charting: Organize information into tables or charts when you need to compare or contrast different aspects of a topic. This method is useful for recording data, statistics, or timelines.

- Highlighting and Annotation: When reading texts or articles, use highlighting or underlining to mark key passages. Additionally, jot down annotations or comments in the margins to capture your thoughts and insights.

- Recording: In situations where you can't take written notes, consider audio recording. Be sure to obtain permission when recording lectures or meetings. Later, you can transcribe the recording or create written summaries.

- Digital Note-Taking: Utilize digital note-taking apps and tools. They offer features like searchability, organization, and the ability to include multimedia elements like images and links. Popular options include Evernote, OneNote, and Notion.

Note-Taking Tips for Success

- Stay Active: Engage with the material actively as you take notes. Paraphrase information in your own words, ask questions, and seek clarity when something is unclear.

- Abbreviate: Develop a set of personal abbreviations or shorthand symbols to write more quickly. This can save time during fast-paced lectures or presentations.

- Review and Revise: Regularly review and revise your notes. Summarize key points, reorganize information, and highlight important details for better retention.

- Date and Organize: Date your notes and keep them organized. Use folders or digital tags to categorize notes by subject or topic.

- Consistency is Key: Maintain a consistent format and style for your notes. This makes it easier to review and compare notes from different sources or sessions.

- Act on Your Notes: Apply the information you've captured in your notes. The act of using the knowledge you've gathered reinforces your memory and understanding.

Efficient note-taking is a skill that evolves with practice. Experiment with different techniques to find the method that works best for your learning style and needs. Whether you're attending lectures, reading books, or participating in meetings, the ability to take effective notes will empower you to make the most of the information you encounter and contribute to your success in various aspects of life.

Chapter 4: Streamlining Your Digital Life

Organizing and Accessing Information

In our interconnected world, managing digital information has become essential. This chapter delves into the art of streamlining your digital life. We explore strategies for organizing and accessing information efficiently, helping you declutter the digital chaos and regain control over your data. From digital file organization to mastering effective search techniques, you'll discover valuable insights to simplify your online existence and harness the power of digital information for productivity and knowledge management.

Digital File Management

In our increasingly digital world, effective digital file management is a vital skill. Whether you're a professional managing work documents, a student organizing study materials, or simply someone trying to declutter your digital life, efficiently managing digital files can save you time, reduce stress, and improve productivity. In this chapter, we explore practical strategies and techniques for organizing and maintaining your digital files effectively.

The Significance of Digital File Management

- Efficient Retrieval: A well-organized file system makes it easy to find the information you need when you need it. No more frustrating searches through a cluttered desktop or multiple folders.

- Productivity Boost: An organized digital workspace promotes productivity. It minimizes distractions and allows you to focus on tasks rather than hunting for files.

- Data Security: Proper file management ensures that your important files are backed up and protected against loss or corruption. It's a crucial aspect of data security.
- Collaboration: In a professional context, organized file systems facilitate collaboration with colleagues or team members. It streamlines the sharing and retrieval of documents.

Practical Digital File Management Techniques

- Use Descriptive Filenames: Give your files descriptive, meaningful names that reflect their content. Avoid vague titles like "Document1" or "Untitled."
- Create Folders: Organize your files into folders or directories based on categories, projects, or subjects. Maintain a clear folder structure to keep related files together.
- Dates and Versioning: Incorporate dates into filenames to indicate when files were created or modified. Use version numbers if

you frequently update files to track revisions.

- Consistent Naming Conventions: Establish consistent naming conventions for files. For example, "YYYY-MM-DD - File Name" can be a structured naming format.

- Cloud Storage: Utilize cloud storage services like Google Drive, Dropbox, or Microsoft OneDrive for convenient and secure file access from any device. These services often include search functionality to find files quickly.

- Metadata and Tags: Assign metadata and tags to your files to enhance searchability. Many operating systems and applications allow you to add keywords or descriptions to files.

- Regular Decluttering: Periodically review and declutter your digital files. Delete outdated or unnecessary files to keep your digital space organized and efficient.

- Backups: Implement a robust backup strategy to safeguard your files. Use external hard drives, cloud backup services, or automatic backup software to ensure data redundancy.

- Search Tools: Master your operating system's search tools. Learn advanced search operators and techniques to quickly locate files using keywords or specific criteria.

- Shortcut Organization: Organize shortcuts and bookmarks on your desktop, taskbar, or browser for easy access to frequently used files, folders, or websites.

- Digital Note-Taking and Documentation: If you take digital notes or maintain documentation, use dedicated note-taking apps or document management systems to keep your notes organized and searchable.

- Email Management: Implement an email filing system to categorize and archive important emails. Regularly clear your inbox to prevent email overload.

- File Metadata Cleaners: Use metadata cleaning tools to remove personal information and hidden data from files before sharing them, ensuring privacy and security.
- Consolidate Duplicates: Identify and consolidate duplicate files to free up storage space and reduce clutter.
- Automate Organization: Explore automation tools and scripts that can help you automate repetitive file management tasks, such as sorting and renaming files.

Efficient digital file management is an ongoing process that requires discipline and commitment. Dedicate time to maintain your digital workspace regularly, and adapt your file organization methods to suit your evolving needs. By implementing these practical strategies, you'll not only declutter your digital life but also streamline your access to information, fostering a more productive and organized digital existence.

Tools and Apps for Information Organization

In the age of information overload, the right tools and apps can be your allies in managing and organizing the digital deluge effectively. Whether you're juggling work-related documents, personal projects, research materials, or simply looking to streamline your digital life, these tools and apps can help you stay organized, boost productivity, and access information with ease. In this chapter, we explore a variety of tools and applications designed to assist you in the art of information organization.

Note-Taking and Documentation Apps

- Evernote: Evernote is a versatile note-taking app that allows you to capture notes, images, web clippings, and audio recordings. It offers powerful search capabilities and the ability to organize notes into notebooks and tags.

- OneNote: Microsoft OneNote is a digital notebook that integrates with the Microsoft Office suite. It offers features like notebooks, sections, and pages for organizing notes and information. You can also collaborate with others in real time.

- Notion: Notion is a highly customizable workspace that combines note-taking, task management, and collaboration. It uses a block-based system that lets you create structured pages for various purposes.

- Obsidian: Obsidian is a note-taking app that emphasizes the interconnection of ideas. It uses backlinks to create a web of connected notes, making it ideal for knowledge management and brainstorming.

File and Document Organization

- Google Drive: Google Drive is a cloud storage and collaboration platform. It offers file organization through folders and includes Google Workspace apps for document creation, editing, and sharing.

- Dropbox: Dropbox is a popular cloud storage service that allows you to store and organize files in the cloud. It also provides file sharing and syncing across devices.

- Microsoft OneDrive: OneDrive is Microsoft's cloud storage solution, integrated with Windows and Office 365. It offers automatic synchronization and file organization features.

- File Explorer/Finder: The built-in file management tools on Windows (File Explorer) and macOS (Finder) provide robust options for organizing files and folders on your computer.

Task and Project Management

- Trello: Trello is a visual project management tool that uses boards, lists, and cards to help you organize tasks and projects. It's particularly useful for teams and collaborative work.

- Asana: Asana is a versatile project management app that allows you to create tasks, assign them to team members, set deadlines, and track progress. It's suitable for both personal and professional use.
- Todoist: Todoist is a task manager and to-do list app that lets you organize tasks by project, due date, and priority. It offers integrations with various platforms and apps.

Information Retrieval and Search

- Google Search: Google's search engine is a powerful tool for quickly finding information on the web. Learn advanced search operators to refine your queries.
- Desktop Search Tools: Use built-in desktop search tools like Windows Search or macOS Spotlight to locate files and applications on your computer quickly.

Bookmark and Link Management

- Pocket: Pocket is a bookmarking app that allows you to save articles, videos, and web pages for later reading. It provides a clutter-free reading experience.

- Instapaper: Instapaper is another app for saving and organizing online content to read later. It offers a distraction-free reading mode.

Password and Login Management

- LastPass: LastPass is a password manager that securely stores your login information and passwords, making it easy to access websites and apps without memorizing multiple credentials.

- 1Password: 1Password offers password management, secure storage for sensitive information, and the ability to generate strong passwords.

Email and Communication Tools

- Email Filters and Labels: Most email clients, such as Gmail and Outlook, offer features like filters and labels to help you organize and prioritize emails.
- Slack: Slack is a team communication tool that allows for organized conversations in channels. It helps reduce email clutter and streamline workplace communication.

These tools and apps cater to various aspects of information organization, from note-taking and file management to task tracking and information retrieval. The key to successful information organization lies in selecting the right tools that align with your specific needs and workflow. Experiment with these applications, adapt them to your preferences, and integrate them into your daily routines to harness their full potential in streamlining your digital life.

Creating a Personalized Information Hub

In our digital age, information is abundant, constantly flowing from various sources, and often overwhelming. To navigate this deluge of data effectively and harness its power, you need a personalized information hub. This hub is a centralized system tailored to your preferences and needs, helping you collect, organize, and access information with ease. In this chapter, we explore the concept of creating a personalized information hub and provide practical steps to build one that enhances your productivity, knowledge management, and overall digital life.

Why You Need a Personalized Information Hub

- Streamlined Access: A personalized hub acts as a one-stop destination for all your information needs. Instead of bouncing between apps and platforms, you have a central location to access content.

- Efficient Organization: With a hub, you can organize information according to your preferences. This customization allows for more efficient sorting and retrieval of data.

- Reduced Overwhelm: The hub helps you manage information overload by curating content based on your interests and priorities, reducing the clutter and noise.

- Enhanced Productivity: By having information at your fingertips, you can work more efficiently and make well-informed decisions.

Building Your Personalized Information Hub

- Choose the Right Platform: Start by selecting a platform or tool that aligns with your needs. It could be a note-taking app, a knowledge management system, or even a customized website or blog.

- Define Your Goals: Clearly outline the purpose of your hub. Are you using it for work-related information, personal interests, research, or a combination? Understanding your goals will guide your customization efforts.

- Curate Your Content: Begin by adding content that matters most to you. This can include articles, documents, research papers, or links to websites. Import or input data into your chosen platform.

- Create Categories or Topics: Organize your content into categories or topics that reflect your interests or work areas. This structure makes it easier to navigate and retrieve information.

- Tagging and Labeling: Use tags or labels to further categorize and identify content. Tags allow for more granular organization and quick access to specific information.

- Customize for Efficiency: Customize your hub's layout and features to suit your workflow. For example, if you're using a note-taking app, set up templates or shortcuts that save time.

- Automation and Integration: Explore automation and integration options. Many tools allow you to connect with other apps or services to streamline content import and updates.

- Regular Updates and Maintenance: Dedicate time for regular updates and maintenance. Remove outdated or irrelevant content, update tags, and ensure your hub remains up-to-date.

Tools for Building Your Information Hub

- Notion: Notion is a versatile tool that allows you to create databases, notes, and pages. It's highly customizable and suitable for a wide range of uses.

- Evernote: Evernote is a note-taking app that offers features like notebooks, tags, and search functionality, making it an excellent choice for information organization.

- Roam Research: Roam Research focuses on connected note-taking, emphasizing the interlinking of ideas. It's ideal for knowledge management and building a personal knowledge graph.

- Personal Website or Blog: Consider creating a personal website or blog where you can curate and share information. Content management systems like WordPress or platforms like Medium are popular choices.

- Feed Readers: For managing news and blog subscriptions, use feed readers like Feedly or Inoreader. They allow you to centralize content from your favorite websites.

- Social Media Aggregators: Tools like TweetDeck for Twitter or aggregators for other social media platforms help you consolidate updates and information from your social networks.

Customization Tips for Efficiency

- Templates: Create templates for common types of content you add to your hub, such as research notes, project plans, or reading lists.

- Keyboard Shortcuts: Master keyboard shortcuts for your chosen platform to navigate and edit content quickly.
- Use Search Efficiently: Learn advanced search operators to find specific content within your hub.
- Backup and Sync: Ensure your hub is backed up regularly and synchronized across devices, so you can access your information from anywhere.
- Share and Collaborate: If needed, set up sharing and collaboration features to work with others on projects or share knowledge.
- Stay Informed: Subscribe to relevant newsletters or RSS feeds to keep your hub updated with the latest information.

Creating a personalized information hub is a dynamic process that evolves with your needs and preferences. It empowers you to take control of your digital life, manage information more efficiently, and stay organized in a world awash with data. By following the steps outlined in this chapter and exploring the recommended tools, you can build a powerful hub that becomes your information sanctuary and a catalyst for productivity and knowledge management.

Chapter 5: Maintaining Balance

Achieving Information Wellness

In our hyper-connected world, the pursuit of information wellness is essential. This chapter explores the delicate balance between staying informed and preventing information overload. We delve into strategies to achieve harmony in your digital life, ensuring that the vast sea of information enriches rather than overwhelms. From mindful information consumption to digital detox techniques, you'll discover insights to foster a healthy relationship with information, preserving mental clarity and well-being in a constantly evolving information landscape.

Avoiding Information Burnout

In our digitally driven world, we have access to a staggering amount of information at our fingertips. While this has its advantages, it also comes with the risk of information burnout. Information burnout occurs when the relentless flow of data overwhelms our cognitive capacity, leading to stress, reduced productivity, and diminished well-being. This chapter explores the causes of information burnout and provides practical strategies to avoid it and maintain a balanced and healthy relationship with information.

Understanding Information Burnout

- Constant Exposure: We live in an era of non-stop information consumption. Emails, social media updates, news alerts, and work-related information flood our screens, leaving little room for respite.

- Multitasking Culture: Many of us engage in constant multitasking, switching between various digital devices and information sources. This can lead to cognitive overload and diminished focus.

- Fear of Missing Out (FOMO): The fear of missing out on important information drives us to check notifications, news, and updates incessantly, even when it's not necessary.

- Information Anxiety: The pressure to stay informed can lead to information anxiety—a constant feeling of unease about missing out or not being up to date.

- Loss of Personal Time: Excessive information consumption can encroach on our personal time, affecting our ability to relax and engage in non-screen activities.

Strategies to Avoid Information Burnout

- Set Information Boundaries: Establish specific time blocks for information consumption. Limit the frequency of email and social media checking to designated periods.

- Unplug Regularly: Dedicate time each day to unplug from digital devices entirely. Engage in offline activities like reading a book, taking a walk, or pursuing a hobby.

- Practice Mindful Consumption: Be mindful of what and how much information you consume. Ask yourself if the information adds value to your life or if it's merely noise.

- Curate Your Information Sources: Be selective about the sources you follow or subscribe to. Choose reliable, high-quality sources that align with your interests and values.

- Use Notification Settings: Customize your device and app notification settings to reduce distractions. Turn off non-essential notifications or set specific quiet hours.

- Digital Detox Days: Designate days where you take a break from all digital devices. Use this time to recharge, connect with nature, or spend quality time with loved ones.

- Prioritize Offline Connections: Foster face-to-face interactions and meaningful conversations with friends and family. These connections provide a valuable break from the digital world.

- Regular Exercise: Engage in physical activity regularly. Exercise has proven benefits for mental well-being and can help reduce stress associated with information overload.

- Limit Multitasking: Focus on one task at a time instead of multitasking. This approach enhances concentration and reduces cognitive overload.

- Information Diet: Practice information fasting by abstaining from information consumption for a set period each day or week. Use this time for reflection or creative pursuits.

- Set Information Goals: Define specific objectives for your information consumption. Determine what you need to know and establish boundaries for what you don't.

- Use Tools Wisely: Utilize productivity apps and tools to streamline information management. Tools like email filters, task managers, and content blockers can help you stay organized.

- Establish a Wind-Down Routine: Create a calming bedtime routine that doesn't involve screens. Reading a physical book or practicing relaxation techniques can improve sleep quality.

- Seek Professional Help: If you feel overwhelmed and experience symptoms of information burnout, such as anxiety or reduced concentration, consider seeking professional help, such as therapy or counseling.

Information burnout is a real challenge in our digital age, but with mindful practices and conscious efforts, you can strike a balance between staying informed and maintaining your well-being. The key is to establish boundaries, prioritize self-care, and be intentional about how you engage with information. By doing so, you can harness the benefits of the digital age while preventing the negative consequences of information overload.

Practicing Digital Detox

In a world dominated by digital devices and constant connectivity, the idea of a digital detox has gained traction as a means of reclaiming our mental well-being and reducing the overwhelming influence of technology in our lives. A digital detox is a deliberate and temporary break from screens, notifications, and the relentless flow of digital information. In this chapter, we explore the importance of digital detox, the benefits it offers, and practical strategies for incorporating it into your life.

Why Digital Detox Matters

- Rest for Overstimulated Minds: Constant exposure to screens and digital information can lead to sensory overload and cognitive fatigue. A digital detox provides your brain with a much-needed break.

- Improved Sleep: The blue light emitted by screens can disrupt sleep patterns. A digital detox before bedtime can lead to better quality sleep and improved overall health.

- Enhanced Productivity: Digital distractions can hinder productivity and focus. Detoxing allows you to regain control of your time and concentration.

- Reconnect with the Physical World: Detoxing encourages you to engage with the physical world, whether through outdoor activities, hobbies, or spending quality time with loved ones.

- Reduced Stress and Anxiety: The constant stream of notifications and information can contribute to stress and anxiety. A digital detox can help alleviate these feelings.

Practical Strategies for a Digital Detox

- Set Clear Goals: Define the purpose and duration of your digital detox. Whether it's a day, a weekend, or a week-long detox, having a clear goal will help you stay committed.

- Notify Contacts: Inform friends, family, and colleagues about your digital detox plans in advance. This prevents misunderstandings and sets expectations.

- Designate Tech-Free Zones: Establish specific areas in your home where digital devices are off-limits. Bedrooms and dining areas are excellent places to start.

- Turn Off Notifications: Disable non-essential notifications on your devices to minimize distractions during your detox period.

- Create a Detox Schedule: Plan your detox periods strategically. Consider incorporating them during weekends or vacations when you have fewer work-related obligations.

- Find Offline Activities: Identify offline activities you enjoy, such as reading physical books, hiking, painting, or playing board games, to fill the time you would typically spend online.

- Digital-Free Mornings and Evenings: Start and end your days without screens. Use this time for reflection, exercise, or to set goals for the day.

- Remove Temptation: During your detox, keep your digital devices out of sight and reach. Consider placing them in a designated "tech drawer" or using apps that lock you out of your phone.

- Practice Mindfulness: Use your detox time to practice mindfulness and meditation. Focus on the present moment and your surroundings.

- Connect with Nature: Spend time in nature by going for walks, hiking, or simply sitting in a park. Nature has a calming effect and can help you recharge.

- Limit Social Media: If you feel overwhelmed by social media, take a break from it. Delete apps or use website blockers to prevent access during your detox.

- Engage in Physical Activity: Regular exercise not only promotes physical health but also boosts mood and reduces stress. Use your detox time for physical activities you enjoy.

- Rediscover Hobbies: Revisit hobbies or interests you've neglected due to digital distractions. Whether it's playing a musical instrument or gardening, rediscover the joy of offline pursuits.

- Read a Physical Book: Reading a physical book can be a calming and enriching experience. Choose a book you've been wanting to read and immerse yourself in its pages.

- Journal Your Experience: Keep a journal during your detox to record your thoughts, emotions, and observations. Reflect on how you feel and the changes you notice.

- Evaluate Your Digital Habits: Use your detox as an opportunity to reflect on your digital habits and consider adjustments that align with your well-being.

A digital detox doesn't have to be an all-or-nothing approach. You can tailor it to your comfort level and needs. The key is to regularly disconnect from screens, engage with the physical world, and reestablish a healthier relationship with technology. Whether it's a short break or an extended detox, these strategies can help you strike a balance between the digital and offline aspects of your life, fostering improved mental and emotional well-being.

Cultivating Mindfulness in Information Consumption

In an age of constant connectivity and digital overload, practicing mindfulness in information consumption is an essential skill for preserving our mental well-being and regaining control over our digital lives. Mindfulness is the practice of being fully present and aware in the moment, and it can be applied to how we consume and interact with information. This chapter explores the concept of mindful information consumption, its benefits, and practical strategies to cultivate it in your daily life.

Why Mindfulness in Information Consumption Matters

Reduced Overwhelm: The digital age bombards us with an endless stream of information, often leading to cognitive overload. Mindful consumption helps filter out noise and reduce overwhelm.

Improved Focus: Mindfulness enhances your ability to concentrate on a single task or piece of information without distraction, leading to increased productivity.

Enhanced Decision-Making: By being fully present in the moment, you can make more informed decisions and avoid impulsive or reactionary responses to information.

Lowered Stress Levels: Mindful information consumption can reduce stress and anxiety associated with information overload and the constant urge to stay connected.

Practical Strategies for Mindful Information Consumption

- Set Intentions: Begin your day with clear intentions about how you want to consume information. Ask yourself what's most important and align your information consumption accordingly.
- Scheduled Check-Ins: Designate specific times during the day for checking email, social media, and news updates. Stick to

these scheduled check-ins rather than reacting to every notification.

- Practice Mindful Breathing: Before diving into digital information, take a few moments to practice mindful breathing. This simple exercise can help center your focus.

- Single-Tasking: Embrace single-tasking instead of multitasking. Focus on one task or piece of information at a time, giving it your full attention.

- Limit Information Sources: Reduce the number of information sources you follow or subscribe to. Be selective about the websites, blogs, and newsletters you engage with.

- Unsubscribe and Unfollow: Regularly review your email subscriptions and social media accounts. Unsubscribe from newsletters and unfollow accounts that don't align with your interests or values.

- Mindful Scrolling: When scrolling through social media or news feeds, be mindful of your reactions and emotions. Pause to reflect on the content's impact before moving on.

- Detox Regularly: Plan regular digital detox periods where you disconnect from screens and digital devices entirely. Use this time for offline activities and reflection.

- Information Triage: When faced with a deluge of information, prioritize what's most relevant and valuable to you. Not everything requires your immediate attention.

- Set Boundaries: Establish clear boundaries for information consumption in your personal and professional life. Communicate these boundaries to others to manage expectations.

- Use Mindful Apps: Consider using mindfulness apps or browser extensions that encourage mindful internet usage. These tools can track your online habits and provide insights into your digital behavior.

- Reflect on Consumption Habits: Periodically reflect on your information consumption habits. Ask yourself how they align with your goals, values, and overall well-being.

- Engage with Slow Media: Seek out slow media sources, such as long-form articles, books, and documentaries, which encourage deeper and more thoughtful engagement.

- Digital Sabbaticals: Plan occasional digital sabbaticals, which are extended periods (e.g., a weekend or a week) of complete disconnection from screens and the digital world.

- Mindful Information Sharing: Before sharing information on social media or in conversations, consider its accuracy, relevance, and potential impact. Avoid spreading misinformation or contributing to information overload.

- Embrace Silence: Embrace moments of digital silence throughout your day. Avoid the urge to fill every idle moment with information consumption.

Cultivating mindfulness in information consumption is an ongoing practice that requires self-awareness and discipline. By integrating these strategies into your daily routine, you can regain control over your digital life, reduce information overwhelm, and create a healthier relationship with the vast sea of information available to you. Mindful information consumption empowers you to harness the benefits of the digital age while preserving your mental clarity and well-being.

Conclusion

The journey through the chapters of "Life Changes with Immediate Impact: How You Get Your Information" has taken us deep into the intricacies of modern information consumption and management. In today's fast-paced digital age, the way we interact with information has transformed our lives in profound ways. From the way we learn and work to the way we stay informed and connected, information has become the driving force behind many of our daily decisions and actions.

In Chapter 1, we explored "The Digital Deluge: Adapting to the Information Onslaught," shedding light on how the sheer volume of information available to us has reshaped our existence. We discovered the importance of adapting to this information onslaught by developing critical skills to filter, process, and manage the vast array of data that confronts us daily.

Chapter 2, "Filtering the Noise: Strategies for Effective Information Selection," offered practical tips on how to sift through the noise and identify reliable sources. We learned the art of discernment in a world overflowing with information, emphasizing the importance of fact-checking and critical thinking.

"Accelerated Learning: Techniques for Rapid Information Absorption" in Chapter 3 unveiled strategies to absorb knowledge swiftly and effectively. We discussed the significance of speed reading, comprehension, and memory techniques, equipping ourselves with tools to become more efficient learners.

Chapter 4, "Streamlining Your Digital Life: Organizing and Accessing Information," took us on a journey to tame the digital chaos. We explored the intricacies of digital file management and discovered the array of tools and apps available to help us organize and access information efficiently.

The culmination of these chapters led us to the realization that personalization is key. In "Creating a Personalized Information Hub" (Chapter 5), we learned the significance of tailoring our information consumption to our unique needs. By curating our digital lives and building personalized information hubs, we can regain control over the data deluge and streamline our digital existence.

However, with great power comes great responsibility. The final chapter, "Maintaining Balance: Achieving Information Wellness," urged us to reflect on the consequences of information overload. We explored the vital importance of mindfulness in information consumption, emphasizing that the pursuit of information wellness is an ongoing journey.

Throughout this exploration, we have discovered that information, in its many forms, can be a double-edged sword. It has the power to empower, educate, and connect us, but it can also overwhelm, distract, and disconnect us from the present moment. The key lies in our ability to adapt, personalize, and be mindful in our information consumption.

As we conclude our journey through these transformative chapters, it's crucial to remember that the digital age continues to evolve. New technologies, platforms, and information sources emerge regularly, shaping the landscape of how we acquire knowledge and connect with the world. The skills and insights we've gained in these chapters will serve as invaluable tools to navigate this ever-changing information landscape.

Ultimately, the way we get our information will continue to change, but the principles of effective information management, discernment, and mindfulness will remain timeless. By mastering these principles, we can not only thrive in the digital age but also maintain a harmonious balance between our digital and offline lives, preserving our well-being, and enhancing our capacity to lead fulfilling and purposeful lives in this information-rich world.